REMARKABLE ———————

RICECAKE

RECIPES

by Janet MacNab

Janet & John MacNab
1658 Bedford Highway
Box 44082, Bedford
Nova Scotia
Canada, B4A 3X5

ISBN 0-9695435 -0-6

Printed & Bound in Nova Scotia, Canada.

INTRODUCTION

I would like to introduce to the public a whole new way of eating. Many people today are looking for an alternative to wheat products, and are having difficulty finding one. Due to allergies suffered by myself and my children, I turned to ricecakes.

We came up with interesting and fun ways to eat them. Many of these recipes are from my children's imagination, and my husband's incredible ability to throw things together and come out with a delicious dish like Lightweight Pizza or Sweety Pie.

Many of these recipes are cooked in the microwave which makes them even more delicious and attractive to serve and you will note that they are usually cooked between 1 - 2 minutes. Having a meal in that length of time is great for busy active people today, whether young or old!

We hope that you will enjoy making these meals we have presented to you in our book. They can be great fun for children and a new experience for adults.

Important Things To Know

Timing

Almost all of the recipes are timed for cooking one ricecake at a time. If you are cooking two ricecakes you will need a little more than double the time.
For example, one ricecake may take 60 seconds (or one minute) to cook, two ricecakes would take about 140 seconds (or two minutes and 20 seconds).

Remember the timing depends on how much you have on your ricecake and how you personally like it cooked. Always start with the shorter cooking time to discover for yourself which time is best for you. You may even like a longer cooking time than is suggested.

There is no standing time with these recipes.

Cheese

In choosing a cheese for these recipes we have found that naturally aged cheese responds best, especially for the microwave recipes. The naturally aged cheese adds flavour and enhances the taste for great, quick meals. Remember always allow the cheese time to cool before eating your ricecake.

Yogurt

We suggest your favourite yogurt for our recipes. Yogurt should be put on the ricecake just before eating it. If it is allowed to sit for any length of time it will make the ricecake soggy.

Vegit

Throughout the book Vegit is also mentioned. It is a delicious substitute for salt and pepper. It is a combination of herbs, spices and vegetables in a powder form. When you taste the rich flavour it adds to almost everything, you will be as delighted as we were to find such a product. It can be purchased in bulk food stores and health food stores.

Spike is also mentioned on a few occasions, it is similar to Vegit but does contain some salt.

Meat

When making recipes that have frankfurters, bologna, etc., we suggest that they be pre-cooked at least one minute before using them. This may not always be necessary, but it does add to the flavour of some recipes.

CONTENTS

Ham Omelet

4 - 6	4 - 6	ricecakes
6 - 12	6 - 12	slices of cheese
15 ml	1 tablespoon	diced onion
4 - 6	4 - 6	eggs
3 -4	3 - 4	diced mushrooms
250 g	1/2 lb	sliced cooked ham
1/2	1/2	medium size diced green pepper

For best results cook one at a time.
Use small microwaveable bowl. e.g. breakfast bowl.

Lightly oil bowl and break egg into it.
Mix well with desired amount of mushrooms, onion, pepper and Vegit.
Cook in microwave for 50 - 60 seconds on HI or until egg is cooked through.
On ricecake place cheese, ham, egg and another slice of cheese.
Cook in microwave for another 30 - 60 seconds on HI or until cheese is melting.

Top with your favourite sauce!
Makes 4 - 6 servings.

Egg Special

4 - 6	4 - 6	ricecakes
250 ml	1 cup	sliced cooked ham
1	1	diced green pepper
1	1	diced onion
8 - 12	8 - 12	sliced mushrooms
500 ml	2 cups	shredded mozzarella cheese
125 ml	1/2 cup	bacon bits
125 ml	1/2 cup	sweet syrup
		Vegit, salt or pepper

Break egg into small microwaveable bowl.
Sprinkle with Vegit or salt and pepper, mix well.
Place mixture in microwave and cook for 50 - 60 seconds on HI or until egg is cooked.
Remove, allow to cool a few minutes.
Place mushroom slices evenly on bottom of small microwaveable dish, approximately 6" round.
Top with diced ham, pepper and onions.
Break ricecake into small pieces, place over mixture.
Sprinkle with bacon bits and shredded cheese.
Place cooked egg over cheese.
Sprinkle with another layer of mushrooms, ham, pepper, onions and cheese.
Place in microwave an cook for 1 1/2 - 2 minutes on HI or until cheese is melting and ingredients are cooked through.

Top with sweet syrup.
Makes 4 - 6 servings.

Poached Egg Bologna Style

4 - 6	4 - 6	ricecakes
4 - 6	4 - 6	eggs
4 - 6	4 - 6	slices of bologna
4 - 6	4 - 6	slices of cheese
		Vegit

Half fill a 9" microwaveable frying pan with water.
Heat water for 2 - 3 minutes on HI in microwave or until water is very hot.
Break egg into water and cook in microwave for 20 - 30 seconds on HI or until egg is cooked.
If desired precook bologna up to 60 seconds in microwave.
Place cooked egg on ricecake and top with a slice of bologna and cheese.
Cook in microwave for 20 - 30 seconds on HI or until cheese is melting.
Sprinkle with Vegit.

Makes 4 - 6 servings.

Yogurt Granola Breakfast

4 - 6	4 - 6	ricecakes
50 - 125 ml	1/4 - 1/2 cup	yogurt
50 - 125 ml	1/4 - 1/2 cup	granola
1/2	1/2	sliced banana
50 ml	1/4 cup	coconut
50 - 125 ml	1/4 - 1/2 cup	peanut butter or honey

Spread honey or peanut butter on each ricecake.
Cover with slices of banana and sprinkle on a thin layer of granola.
Top with a spoonful of yogurt and some coconut.

What a breakfast!
Makes 4 - 6 servings.

Mushroom Omelet

4 - 6	4 - 6	ricecakes
6 - 12	6 - 12	slices of cheese
125 ml	1/2 cup	diced onions
4 - 6	4 - 6	eggs
4 - 6	4 - 6	sliced mushrooms
1	1	diced green pepper
		Vegit

Egg Mixture:

Lightly oil 4-6 small microwave bowls approximately
6" round by 1" deep. (vegetable oil spray preferably).
Place one egg in each bowl and beat slightly.
Sprinkle in desired amount of onions, peppers, mushrooms and
Vegit. Mix with fork.
Place each bowl separately in microwave and cook for 1 to 1 1/2
minutes on high temperature.

Ricecake:

Cover surface of each ricecake with cheese.
Place cooked omelet on next. Top with one or two slices of
cheese.
Reheat in microwave for 20-30 seconds on high or until cheese
is melting.
Remove and allow to cool before eating.

What a breakfast, lunch or snack!
Makes 4 - 6 servings.

Egg & Ham Breakfast

4 - 6	4 - 6	ricecakes
2 - 3	2 - 3	sliced mushrooms
4 - 6	4 - 6	sliced ham - cooked
8 - 12	8 - 12	slices of cheese
		Vegit

Oil small microwaveable bowl.
Break egg into bowl, mix well with Vegit.
Cook in microwave for 60 -70 seconds on HI or until egg is cooked.
Place slice of cheese on each ricecake.
Top with cooked egg and a slice of ham.
Arrange mushrooms over ham and top with another slice of cheese.
Sprinkle with Vegit.
Heat in microwave for 40 - 60 seconds on HI or until cheese is melting.

Remember, it will be hot!
Makes 4 - 6 servings.

Morning Bologna

4 - 6	4 - 6	ricecakes
4 - 6	4 - 6	sliced bologna
6 - 12	6 - 12	slices of cheese
1/2	1/2	diced green pepper
1/2	1/2	diced onion

Place a slice of cheese and bologna on each ricecake.
Sprinkle on desired amount of pepper and onion.
Top with another slice of cheese and cook in microwave for 50-60 seconds on HI or until cheese is melting.

Makes 4 to 6 servings.

Bacon & Eggs Sunnyside Up

4 - 6	4 - 6	ricecakes
2 - 3	2 - 3	strips of bacon
4 - 6	4 - 6	eggs
		ketchup
		Vegit

Oil medium size microwaveable bowl. e.g. regular size cereal bowl.
Break egg into bowl, poke hole in egg yoke.
Cover with plastic wrap.
Cook in microwave for 60 - 90 seconds on HI or until egg is cooked.
Place bacon on roasting rack or on microwave dish.
Cover with paper towel and cook on HI for 2 - 3 minutes.
Place cooked egg on ricecake.
Cut bacon into small pieces, place on egg.
If desired, heat for 40 seconds in microwave on HI.
Sprinkle with Vegit and top with ketchup or your favourite topping.

Makes 4 - 6 servings.

Poached Egg Delight

4 - 6	4 - 6	ricecakes
4 - 6	4 - 6	eggs
		Vegit

Half fill a 9" microwaveable frying pan with water.
Heat water for 2 - 3 minutes on HI in microwave, or until water is very hot.
Break egg into water and cook in microwave for 20 - 30 seconds on HI or until egg is cooked.
Place cooked egg on ricecake and sprinkle with Vegit and top with your favourite sauce.

Makes 4 - 6 servings.

Upside Down Egg

4 - 6	4 - 6	ricecakes
125 g	1/4 lb	cooked sliced ham
2	2	diced celery sticks
1	1	diced onion
3 - 6	3 - 6	eggs
4 - 6	4 - 6	diced mushrooms
		Vegit & garlic powder

Combine diced ham, onions, celery and mushrooms in mixing bowl. Break 2 - 3 eggs into a separate bowl. Sprinkle with Vegit, garlic powder and stir well.

Place 1 or 2 ricecakes on separate microwaveable plates. Pour some egg mixture over each ricecake. Top with ham, onions and celery. Pour remaining mixture over each ricecake. Allow egg to cover ham, onions and celery topping. Let it freely run over the sides of each ricecake.

Cook each ricecake in microwave for 60 - 80 seconds on HI or until egg and mixture is completely cooked.

Surprisingly tasty. Makes 4 - 6 servings.

Fruit Fibre Rainbow Treat

4 - 6	4 - 6	ricecakes
4 - 6	4 - 6	cherries
50 - 125 ml	1/4 - 1/2 cup	yogurt
50 - 125 ml	1/4 - 1/2 cup	fruit fibre cereal
50 - 125 ml	1/4 - 1/2 cup	cream cheese
50 ml	1/4 cup	rainbow sprinkles
125 ml	1/2 cup	currants or chopped dates
1 - 2	1 - 2	sliced bananas or apples

Spread ricecakes with generous amount of cream cheese.
Top with bananas, cereal and dates.
Dab on desired amount of yogurt and sprinkle on rainbow sprinkles.

Great fun for breakfast! Makes 4 - 6 servings.

Egg Over Ricecake

4 - 6	4 - 6	ricecakes
4 - 6	4 - 6	slices of cheese
250 g	1/2 lb	diced ham or bologna
1	1	diced green pepper
125 ml	1/4 lb	smoked meat
4	4	eggs

Break all eggs into bowl, mix well.
Place each ricecake on small microwaveable dish.
Pour half of the egg mixture over each ricecake.
Sprinkle on ham and pepper.
Pour on remaining half of egg mixture.
Top with smoked meat and cheese.
Cook each ricecake for 2 minutes on HI or until egg mixture is cooked.

A different way to eat eggs!
Makes 4 - 6 servings.

Ham & Egg Special

4 - 6	4 - 6	ricecakes
4 - 6	4 - 6	eggs
2 - 3	2 - 3	sliced tomatoes
4 - 6	4 - 6	sliced ham - cooked
2 - 4	2 - 4	sliced mushrooms
4 - 6	4 - 6	slices of cheese
		Vegit

For best results cook one at a time.
Break one egg into bowl and mix well with Vegit.
Pour into 7" microwaveable dish - sprayed with oil.
Cook in microwave for two minutes on HI.
Break ricecake into small bite-size pieces and place on egg.
Top with sliced ham, mushroom, tomato and cheese.
Cook in microwave for another 40 - 60 seconds or until cheese is melting.

Sweet syrup taste great over this special.
Makes 4 - 6 servings.

Banana Cereal Breakfast

1	1	ricecake
1	1	sliced banana
15 ml	1 tablespoon	chopped dates
15 ml	1 tablespoon	sesame seeds
15 ml	1 tablespoon	shredded coconut

Break ricecake into small pieces in cereal bowl, add sliced
bananas, sesame seeds and dates.
Sprinkle with coconut.
Pour in milk.

Makes a hearty breakfast!
Makes one serving.

Granola Cereal Breakfast

1	1	ricecake
125 ml	1/2 cup	granola
1	1	sliced apple
5 ml	1 teaspoon	honey
125 ml	1/2 cup	milk or
1	1 - 200 ml	drinking yogurt

Break ricecake into small pieces in cereal bowl.
Mix with apple slices and granola.
Pour in desired amount of milk or yogurt drink.
Top with honey.

Great way to get you through the morning!
Makes one serving.

Cheese & Tomato Lunch

4 - 6	4 - 6	ricecakes
4 - 6	4 - 6	slices of marble cheese
1 - 2	1 - 2	sliced tomatoes
2 - 3	2 - 3	shredded romaine lettuce leaves
50 ml	1/4 cup	mayonnaise
50 ml	1/4 cup	sour cream

Spread mayonnaise on each ricecake.
Place shredded lettuce and tomatoes evenly over surface.
Sprinkle with Vegit and top with another slice of cheese.
Heat in microwave for 40-60 seconds on HI or until cheese is bubbling and melting.
Allow to cool, top with a spoonful of sour cream.

Makes 4 - 6 servings.

Spinach Salad Lunch

4 - 6	4 - 6	ricecakes
3 - 4	3 - 4	hard boiled eggs
2 - 4	2 - 4	spinach leaves
125 ml	1/2 cup	grated cheese
125 ml	1/2 cup	cooked diced ham
50 ml	1/4 cup	mayonnaise

Spread a thin layer of mayonnaise on each ricecake.
Cut spinach into bite-size pieces and arrange over ricecakes.
Sprinkle on grated cheese.
Slice eggs and arrange over cheese.
Sprinkle on desired amount of ham and a little more cheese.
Top with desired amount of your favourite dressing.

What a delight!
Makes 4 - 6 servings.

Frankfurter Special

4 - 6	4 - 6	ricecakes
4 - 6	4 - 6	sliced mushrooms
4 - 6	4 - 6	sliced frankfurters
8 - 12	8 - 12	slices of cheese
		Vegit

Place 1 slice of cheese on each ricecake to cover surface.
Add sliced frankfurters, mushrooms.
Sprinkle with Vegit.
Top with another slice of cheese.
Heat in microwave for 40-60 seconds on high.
Allow to cool and serve.

Makes 4 - 6 servings.

Microdog

4 - 6	4 - 6	ricecakes
4 - 6	4 - 6	slices of cheese
4	4	sliced wieners

Place one slice of cheese on each ricecake to cover surface.
Arrange sliced wieners loosely on cheese.
Heat each ricecake in microwave for 40 - 60 seconds on HI or
until wieners are cooked and cheese is slightly melted.
Allow to cool a little before serving.
Tastes great with relish, mustard, ketchup etc...

Try a little sauerkraut!
Makes 4 - 6 servings.

Ham & Celery Munch

4 - 6	4 - 6	ricecakes
125 ml	1/2 cup	shredded cheese (your favourite)
2	2	diced celery stocks
6 - 8	6 - 8	sliced cooked ham
1	1	diced onion

Cover surface of each ricecake with cheese and diced ham.
Sprinkle celery and onions evenly over surface.
Heat each ricecake in microwave for 20-40 seconds on high or
until cheese is melted.

Tastes great with your favourite sauce or dressing!
Makes 4 - 6 servings.

Crunchy Lunch

4 - 6	4 - 6	ricecakes
8 - 12	8 - 12	slices of salami
4 - 6	4 - 6	slices of cheese
50 ml	1/4 cup	mayonnaise
1/2	1/2	sliced cucumber

Spread ricecakes with mayonnaise.
Top with salami, cucumber and cheese.
Heat in microwave for 40-60 seconds on HI or until
cheese is melting.

Hot or cold it's a great lunch.
Makes 4 - 6 servings.

Shawn's Rice Lunch

4 - 6	4 - 6	ricecakes
250 ml	1 cup	cooked rice
125 ml	1/2 cup	curry sauce

Place desired amount of rice on each ricecake.
Heat in microwave for 20-30 seconds on HI or until
heated through.
Top with dab of curry sauce.
Great way to eat leftover cooked rice.

See "Sauces" section for instant curry sauce.

Makes 4 - 6 servings.

Jack's Fish Fingers

4 - 6	4 - 6	ricecakes
4 - 6	4 - 6	cheese slices - Monterey Jack with caraway
12 - 18	12 - 18	fishsticks, pre-cooked
50 ml	1/4 cup	tartar sauce

Place cheese on ricecakes, to cover surface.
Top each with 3-4 fishsticks, or fishfingers.
Heat each ricecake for 30-40 seconds on HI or until
fish is heated through.
Dab on desired amount of tartar sauce.

See "Sauces" section for homemade tartar sauce.

Makes 4 - 6 servings.

Instant Grilled Cheese

4 - 6	4 - 6	ricecakes
8 - 12	8 - 12	cheese slices

Place 1-2 slices of cheese on each ricecake to cover surface.
Heat in microwave for 20-30 seconds on HI or until cheese is
bubbling and melting.

To heat four at a time: 90-110 seconds on HI.
Cooking time will vary according to the kind of cheese and
thickness of cheese used.
For extra flavour sprinkle with your favourite spices.

Makes 4 - 6 servings.

Cole Slaw Dish

4 - 6	4 - 6	ricecakes
1	1 cup	cole slaw
125 ml	1/2 cup	cottage cheese

Spread cottage cheese on each ricecake.
Top with desired amount of cole slaw.

Fast light lunch!
Makes 4 - 6 servings.

Ham Plateau

4 - 6	4 - 6	ricecakes
4 - 6	4 - 6	slices of cheese
4 - 6	4 - 6	sliced cooked ham
4 - 6	4 - 6	sliced mushrooms
1/2	1/2	diced green pepper
1	1	sliced cucumber (small)
1	1	diced onion

Place a slice of cheese on each ricecake to cover surface.
Top with a slice of ham and cucumber.
Sprinkle on onions, pepper, mushrooms and Vegit.
Tastes great hot or cold.

To serve hot: heat each ricecake in microwave for 30-40 seconds
on HI or until heated through.

Makes 4 - 6 servings.

Instant Granola Yogurt

4 - 6	4 - 6	ricecakes
2	2 - 125 g	containers of yogurt with granola

Lightly butter ricecakes.
Spread generous amount of yogurt over each.
Top with granola.

Makes 4 - 6 servings.

Jared's Alfalfa Brunch

4 - 6	4 - 6	ricecakes
4 - 6	4 - 6	sliced bologna
125 ml	1/2 cup	alfalfa sprouts
250 g	1/2 lb	slices of marble cheese

Place a slice of cheese on each ricecake and arrange desired amount of alfalfa sprouts on next.
Top with a slice of bologna and another slice of cheese.
Heat each ricecake in microwave for 60-90 seconds on HI or until cheese is melting.
If desired pre-cook bologna for 60 seconds on HI.

A very simple and easy lunch for young and old!
Makes 4 - 6 servings.

Cheese & Egg Lunch

4 - 6	4 - 6	ricecakes
4 - 6	4 - 6	eggs
6 - 12	6 - 12	slices of cheese
		Vegit

Lightly oil small microwaveable bowl.
e.g. approximately the size of a regular cereal bowl.
Break one egg into bowl and poke a small hole in egg yoke.
Cover with plastic wrap and cook in microwave for
60-90 seconds on HI or until cooked through.
Place a slice of cheese on each ricecake.
Top with cooked egg and sprinkle with Vegit.
Place another slice of cheese on top.
Cook for 50-70 seconds on HI or until cheese is bubbly and melting slightly.
Dab on a little ketchup or sauce.

Makes 4 - 6 servings.

Egg Salad

4 - 6	4 - 6	ricecakes
3 - 4	3 - 4	hard boiled eggs
50 ml	1/4 cup	mayonnaise
2 - 3	2 - 3	shredded romaine lettuce leaves
30 ml	1-2 tablespoons	Italian salad dressing
		Vegit

Remove shells from hard boiled eggs.
Place in large bowl add mayonnaise, Italian dressing and Vegit, mix well.
Spread mayonnaise on ricecakes and top with shredded lettuce and desired amount of egg mixture.
Sprinkle with Vegit.

Makes 4 - 6 servings.

Gouda & Mushroom

4 - 6	4 - 6	ricecakes
8 - 12	8 - 12	sliced mushrooms
250 g	1/2 lb	gouda cheese

Cover surface of ricecake with cheese.
Top with sliced mushrooms and a little more cheese.
Heat in microwave on HI for 30-40 seconds or until cheese is melting.
Allow to cool a few minutes before eating.

Makes 4 - 6 servings.

Western Ricecake

4 - 6	4 - 6	ricecakes
8 - 12	8 - 12	slices of cheese
3 - 4	3 - 4	sliced mushrooms
4 - 6	4 - 6	eggs
3 - 4	3 - 4	sliced frankfurters
		Vegit

Spray regular size microwaveable bowl with oil. e.g. regular size breakfast bowl. Break one egg into bowl and sprinkle with Vegit. Add desired amount of frankfurters and mushrooms and mix well. Place cooked egg on ricecake. Heat in microwave for 40-50 seconds on HI or until egg is cooked.
Try one of our instant sauces on top.

Makes 4 - 6 servings.

Ricecake Pizza

4 - 6	4 - 6	ricecakes
150 ml	1/2 cup	diced pepperoni
250 ml	1 cup	shredded mozzarella cheese
50 - 125 ml	1/4 - 1/2 cup	pizza sauce
4 - 6	4 - 6	sliced mushrooms
4 - 6	4 - 6	sliced olives
1/2	1/2	diced green pepper

Cover surface of each ricecake with cheese.
Top with diced pepperoni, pepper, mushrooms, olives and another slice of cheese.
Place each ricecake in microwave and cook for 40-60 seconds on HI or until cooked through and cheese is melting.
Heat pizza sauce for approximately 1 minute and spoon over cooked ricecake.

A great fast, easy pizza!
Makes 4 - 6 servings.

18

Salad Ricecake Supreme

4 - 6	4 - 6	ricecakes
4 - 6	4 - 6	sliced mushrooms
4 - 6	4 - 6	sliced cooked ham
2 - 4	2 - 4	shredded romaine lettuce leaves
8 - 12	8 - 12	slices of cheese
1	1	diced green pepper
1	1	diced small onion
50 ml	1/4 cup	mayonnaise

Spread ricecake with mayonnaise and top with shredded lettuce and a slice of ham. Sprinkle with diced pepper, onions and mushrooms. Top with another slice of cheese.
Heat each ricecake in microwave for 40-60 seconds on HI or until cheese is bubbling and melting.

Can be eaten hot or cold.
Makes 4 - 6 servings.

Bacon & Cheese Break

4 - 6	4 - 6	ricecakes
2 - 3	2 - 3	strips of bacon
1 - 2	1 - 2	sliced tomatoes
4 - 6	4 - 6	slices of cheese
1	1	diced onion
		Vegit

Pre-cook bacon in microwave for 2-3 minutes on HI or until bacon is fully cooked.
Place cheese on ricecake, to cover surface.
Cut bacon into bite-size pieces and arrange over cheese.
Top with tomatoes, onions and Vegit.
Heat EACH ricecake in microwave for 40-60 seconds on HI or until cooked through.

Makes 4 - 6 servings.

Cauliflower Jack

4 - 6	4 - 6	ricecakes
1/2	1/2	medium size cauliflower
250 g	1/2 lb	Monterey Jack cheese with caraway

Place a slice of cheese on each ricecake to cover surface.
Break cauliflower into small pieces and place on next.
Top with another slice of cheese.
Heat in microwave for 30-40 seconds on HI or until cheese is melting.
Allow to cool a few minutes before eating.
Holds in great taste of cauliflower.

Makes 4 - 6 servings.

Ricecake Salad

4 - 6	4 - 6	ricecakes
1	1	sliced cucumber (medium)
4 - 5	4 - 5	romaine lettuce leaves
2 - 4	2 - 4	sliced mushrooms
50 ml	1/4 cup	shredded cheese
2 - 3	2 - 3	sliced tomatoes
50 ml	1/4 cup	mayonnaise
		Vegit

Spread a thin layer of mayonnaise on each ricecake.
Cut lettuce leaves into bite-size pieces and place on next.
Top with cucumber, tomato and mushroom slices.
Sprinkle with Vegit and desired amount of shredded cheese.
Try a light mayonnaise.

Makes dieting a joy!
Makes 4 - 6 servings.

Kiwi Light

4 - 6	4 -6	ricecakes
2 - 3	2 - 3	sliced kiwi
125 ml	1/2 cup	yogurt
50 ml	1/4 cup	cream cheese
125 ml	1/2 cup	chopped walnuts

Spread cream cheese on each ricecake.
Place kiwi slices on evenly.
Sprinkle with chopped walnuts.
Top with a spoonful of yogurt and another slice of kiwi.

Variation: try your favourite kind of nut.

Makes 4 - 6 servings.

Cheeze Whiz & Sweet Pickles

4 - 6	4 - 6	ricecakes
125 ml	1/2 cup	cheeze whiz
3 - 6	3 - 6	sweet pickle slices

Spread desired amount of cheeze whiz on each ricecake.
Slice pickles and place on cheese.
Sprinkle with a small amount of Vegit.
Serve cold.

Makes a great afternoon snack!
Makes 4 - 6 servings.

Lightweight Pizza

4 - 6	4 - 6	ricecakes
250 ml	1 cup	diced pepperoni
250 ml	1 cup	diced salami
750 ml	3 cups	shredded mozzarella cheese
1 - 2	1 - 2	diced small onions
1	1	diced green pepper
1	1	diced red pepper
750 ml	3 cups	sliced mushrooms
125 ml	1/2 cup	sliced olives
50 ml	1/4 cup	pizza spices (optional)
250 ml	1 cup	pizza sauce

Place sliced mushrooms evenly on the bottom of 4-6 microwaveable dishes approximately 6" round by 1" deep.
Sprinkle desired amount of onions and peppers over mushrooms.
Cover with layers of pepperoni and shredded cheese.
Crumple ricecake over cheese, spread evenly.
Sprinkle with desired amount of pizza spices, onions and peppers.
Cover surface with diced salami.
Top with sliced mushrooms, olives and cheese.
Cook EACH dish in microwave for 2-3 minutes on high.

Makes a nice light pizza!
Makes 4-6 servings.

Pizza Egg

4 - 6	4 - 6	ricecakes
250 ml	1 lb	slices of mozzarella cheese
125 ml	1/2 lb	diced salami or pepperoni
4 - 6	4 - 6	eggs
8 - 10	8 - 10	diced mushrooms
250 ml	1 cup	pizza sauce
50 ml	1/4 cup	pizza spices
1	1	diced green pepper
1	1	diced onion

Oil medium size microwaveable bowl. e.g. regular size breakfast bowl. Break one egg into bowl and sprinkle in desired amount of pizza spices, mix well. Cook in microwave for 50-60 seconds on HI or until egg is cooked through. Place a slice of cheese on each ricecake. Top with cooked egg, salami, onions, mushrooms and pepper. Cover ingredients with another slice or slices of cheese. Cook in microwave for 40-60 seconds on HI or until heated through and cheese is melting.
Remove and top with desired amount of pizza sauce.

What a combo!
Makes 4 - 6 servings.

Vegit Away

1 - 2	1 - 2	ricecakes
		Vegit

Spread a thin layer of butter on both sides of ricecake.
Break into small pieces and place in bowl.
Sprinkle with Vegit, mix.
Heat in microwave 20-40 seconds on HI or until ricecake is heated through and butter is dissolved.

Great alternative to popcorn!
Makes one serving

Pineapple Pizza

4 - 6	4 - 6	ricecakes
284 ml	10 oz	can pineapple bits
1/2	1/2	diced sweet, red pepper
250 g	1/2 lb	slices of mozzarella cheese
250 g	1/2 lb	diced pepperoni
		pizza spices

Place cheese over surface of ricecakes.
Drain pineapple and spread evenly over cheese.
Sprinkle with pepperoni, pepper, mushrooms and pizza spices.
Top with another slice of cheese.
Heat each ricecake for 40-60 seconds on HI or until cooked through and cheese is melting.

Makes 4 - 6 servings.

Mango Pizza

4 - 6	4 - 6	ricecakes
1 - 398 ml	1 - 14 oz	can sliced mangos or 2 fresh mangos
2 - 3	2 - 3	sliced mushrooms
50 ml	1/4 cup	bacon bits
6 - 12	6 - 12	mozzarella cheese slices
50 ml	1/4 cup	pizza spices

Cover surface of each ricecake with mozzarella cheese.
Place thinly sliced mangos on cheese, sprinkle with bacon bits and pizza spices.
Top with sliced mushrooms and another layer of cheese.
Place each ricecake pizza on plate and heat in microwave for 40-60 seconds or until cheese is bubbling and melting slightly.
Remove and allow to cool a few minutes before eating.

Makes 4 - 6 servings.

Black Forest Delight

4 - 6	4 - 6	ricecakes
4 - 6	4 - 6	slices black forest ham
1	1	diced sweet pepper
1	1	diced onion
3 - 4	3 - 4	sliced mushrooms
50 ml	1/4 cup	sour cream

Cover surface of ricecake with cheese.
Top with a slice of ham, mushrooms, pepper and onions.
Optional: Top with another slice of cheese.
Heat EACH ricecake for 30-40 seconds on HI in microwave or
until heated through and cheese is melting slightly.
Dab on sour cream.

Makes 4 - 6 servings.

Roast Beef Dish

4 - 6	4 - 6	ricecakes
248 ml	10 oz can	prepared gravy
4 - 6	4 - 6	slices of cooked roast beef
250 ml	1 cup	cooked rice
3 - 4	3 - 4	sliced mushrooms
1	1	diced onion

Place each ricecake on a small dish.
Cut roast beef into bite-size pieces and place on ricecake.
Top with rice, onions, mushrooms.
Heat EACH ricecake in microwave for 1-1 1/2 minutes on HI or
until heated through.
Pour desired amount of heated gravy over each.

Eat with fork and knife.

Makes 4 - 6 servings.

Big Al's Donair

8 - 10	8 - 10	ricecakes
2 - 3	2 - 3	diced tomatoes
2 - 3	2 - 3	diced onions
500 kg	1 lb	sliced donair meat
250 ml	1 cup	donair sauce
500 m	2 cups	sliced mushrooms
500 kg	1 lb	shredded mozzarella cheese

Dishes needed: 8-10 microwaveable dishes 6" by 1" deep.

Cover bottom of each dish with sliced mushrooms.
Sprinkle on onions, tomatoes and a layer of shredded cheese.
Break ricecake into small pieces and place on cheese.
Sprinkle on another layer of onions, tomatoes, mushrooms and bite-size pieces of donair meat.
Cover with another layer of cheese and desired amount of sauce.
Heat EACH dish in microwave for 2-3 minutes on HI or until cheese is bubbling and melting slightly.
Serve hot, but be careful!

What a donair!
Makes 8 - 10 servings.

Pizz - It

1	1	ricecake
1 - 2	1 - 2	slices of cheese
		pizza spices

Cover surface of ricecake with cheese.
Sprinkle with desired amount of pizza spices.
Heat in microwave for 20-30 seconds on HI or until
cheese is melting slightly.

Makes one serving.

Egg Roll Sideorder

| 1 | 1 | ricecake |
| | | egg roll seasoning |

Spread butter on ricecake and sprinkle with egg roll seasoning.
e.g. Red Dragon
Heat for 15-20 seconds on HI or until ricecake is warm.

Makes one serving.

Garlic Spread

| 1 | 1 | ricecake |
| | | garlic spread |

Cover ricecake with garlic spread.
Heat in microwave for 15-20 seconds on HI or until spread has
melted into ricecake.

Great with pasta!
Makes one serving.

Mini Donair

4 - 6	4 - 6	ricecakes
1/2	1/2	diced sweet, red pepper
1/2	1/2	diced green pepper
125 - 250 ml	1/2 - 1 cup	donair sauce
500 kg	1 lb	donair slices
1	1	diced onion
50 ml	1/4 cup	cream cheese
125 ml	1/2 cup	grated mozzarella cheese
1	1	diced tomato

Spread cream cheese on each ricecake.
Cut donair meat into bite-size pieces and place on ricecakes.
Top with diced pepper, tomato and shredded cheese.
Pour on desired amount of donair sauce.
Heat EACH ricecake for 40-60 seconds on HI or until heated through.

Makes 4 - 6 servings.

Corned Beef On RI

4 - 6	4 - 6	ricecakes
8 - 12	8 - 12	sliced corned beef
250 ml	1 cup	sauerkraut
8 - 12	8 - 12	slices of cheese

Cover surface of each ricecake with cheese.
Cut meat into bite-size pieces and place on ricecake.
Spread sauerkraut evenly over meat.
Top with a slice of cheese.
Heat EACH ricecake for 40-60 seconds on high or until cheese is melting.
Allow a few minutes to cool before eating.

Makes 4 - 6 servings.

Eggdog

4 - 6	4 - 6	ricecakes
4 - 6	4 - 6	eggs
6 - 12	6 - 12	slices of marble cheese
1	1	diced green pepper
2 - 3	2 - 3	diced mushrooms
2 - 4	2 - 4	sliced wieners
		pizza spices
		Vegit

Lightly oil medium size microwaveable bowl.
e.g. regular size breakfast bowl.
Break egg into bowl and mix with pizza spices and Vegit.
Cook each egg in microwave for 50 - 60 seconds on HI or until egg is cooked.
Place a slice of cheese on each ricecake and top with cooked egg, wieners, pepper and mushrooms.
Sprinkle with pizza spices and Vegit and top with another slice of cheese.
Cook each ricecake in microwave for 40 - 60 seconds on HI or until cheese is melting.

Makes 4 - 6 servings.

B.B.Q. Flavour

1	1	ricecake
		barbecue spices

Spread ricecake with butter or margarine.
Sprinkle with desired amount of barbecue spices.
Heat for 15-20 seconds on HI in microwave.

Goes great with barbecuing.

Strawberry Whip

4 - 6	4 - 6	ricecakes
250 ml	1 pkg	whipped topping
50 ml	1/4 cup	graham wafer crumbs
375 ml	1 1/2 cups	strawberries

Whip up topping according to directions on package.
When near the end of whipping stage, slowly add graham wafer crumbs until well blended.
Place one layer of topping on each ricecake.
Drop desired amount of strawberries into topping.
Top with another spoonful of topping and strawberries.

Try a low calorie whipped topping!

Variation: *Great with blueberries or raspberries.*

Makes 4 - 6 servings.

Cheesy Apricot

4 - 6	4 - 6	ricecakes
1 - 398 ml	1 - 14 oz	apricot halves (4 fresh apricots)
50 ml	1/4 cup	cottage cheese
50 ml	1/4 cup	cream cheese
50 ml	1/4 cup	rainbow coconut

Spread a layer of cream cheese and then a layer of cottage cheese on each ricecake.
Slice apricots into thin slices and place evenly over cottage cheese.
Sprinkle with coconut.

Quick and tasty!
Makes 4 - 6 servings.

Mincemeat Pie Ricecake

4 - 6	4 - 6	ricecakes
125 ml	1/2 cup	mincemeat
125 ml	1/2 cup	ice cream
50 ml	1/4 cup	cream cheese

Spread cream cheese on each ricecake.
Top with desired amount of mincemeat.
Heat in microwave for 30-40 seconds on HI or until heated through.
Top with your favourite ice cream.
Eat right away.

Makes 4 - 6 servings.

Mincemeat & Apple Pie

4 - 6	4 - 6	ricecakes
125 ml	1/2 cup	mincemeat
1 - 2	1 - 2	sliced apples
125 ml	1/2 cup	yogurt
50 ml	1/4 cup	cream cheese

Spread cream cheese on each ricecake.
Add desired amount of mincemeat.
Arrange apple slices on top.
Heat in microwave for 30-40 seconds on HI or until heated through.
Top with your favourite yogurt.
Can also be served cold.

Makes 4 - 6 servings.

Cherry Pear Pie

4 - 6	4 - 6	ricecakes
125 ml	1/2 cup	cherry pie filling
50 ml	1/4 cup	currants or raisins
50 ml	1/4 cup	pear pie filling
125 ml	1/2 cup	cream cheese

Spread generous amount of cream cheese over each ricecake.
Top with cherry pie filling and make small hole in centre.
Place a small amount of pear filling into centre.
Sprinkle with raisins and coconut.
Heat each ricecake in microwave for 20-40 seconds on HI or until pie is warmed through.

Also tastes great cold!
Makes 4 - 6 servings.

Cottage Cheese Fruit Pie

4 - 6	4 - 6	ricecakes
250 ml	1 cup	cottage cheese
1	1	sliced banana
1	1	sliced peach
2	2	sliced plums
4 - 6	4 - 6	grapes

Spread a layer of cottage cheese on each ricecake.
Top with sliced bananas, peaches and plums.
Spread on another layer of cottage cheese.
Top with a grape.
Serve Cold.

Great summer delight!
Makes 4 - 6 servings.

Lemon Coconut Pie

4 - 6	4 - 6	ricecakes
250 ml	1 cup	lemon pie filling
2	2	sliced bananas
4 - 6	4 - 6	whole cherries
50 ml	1/4 cup	granola
50 ml	1/4 cup	cream cheese
50 ml	1/4 cup	shredded coconut (optional)

Spread cream cheese on each ricecake.
Top with desired amount of lemon pie filling and arrange banana slices next.
Sprinkle with granola and coconut.
Top with a cherry.
Serve cold or heat each ricecake in microwave for 20-30 seconds on HI.

A pie in a minute!
Makes 4 - 6 servings.

Blueberry Pie Ricecake

4 - 6	4 - 6	ricecakes
250 ml	1 cup	blueberry pie filling
250 ml	1 cup	whipped cream
50 - 125 ml	1/4 - 1/2 cup	cream cheese

Spread generous amount of cream cheese over each ricecake.
Top with desired amount of blueberry pie filling and whipped cream.
A few more blueberries or a teaspoon of blueberry pie filling makes a great topping.
If desired, heat each ricecake for 20-30 seconds on HI before adding whipped cream or eat as is.

Makes 4 - 6 servings.

Fruit Cocktail

4 - 6	4 - 6	ricecakes
398 ml	14 oz can	fruit cocktail
50 ml	1/4 cup	cream cheese
250 ml	1 cup	whipped topping

Spread cream cheese on each ricecake.
Drain fruit cocktail, and spoon on desired amount.
Top with whipped topping.

Makes 4 - 6 servings.

Rice Crisp

4 - 6	4 - 6	ricecakes
125 ml	1/2 cup	marshmallow fluff
375 ml	1 1/2 cups	Rice Krispies

Mix one (1) cup of Rice Krispies with marshmallow fluff.
Spread on ricecakes and sprinkle with remaining Rice Krispies.

Variation: *Spread ricecake with marshmallow fluff and top with Rice Krispies.*

Makes 4 - 6 servings.

Desserts

Apple Cinnamon

4 - 6	4 - 6	ricecakes
50 - 125 ml	1/4 - 1/2 cup	cream cheese or cinnamon spread
1	1	sliced apple
50 ml	1/4 cup	shredded coconut
125 ml	1/2 cup	broken walnuts
250 ml	1 cup	yogurt

Spread cream cheese or cinnamon spread over each ricecake.
Arrange slices of apple evenly over spread.
Top with walnuts and coconut.
Eat as is or heat in microwave for 40-60 seconds on HI or until heated through.

Top with your favourite yogurt!
Makes 4 - 6 servings.

Instant Cheesecake

4 - 6	4 - 6	ricecakes
250 ml	1 cup	cherry pie filling
50 ml	1/4 cup	cream cheese
50 ml	1/4 cup	graham wafer crumbs
250 ml	1 cup	whipped topping

Spread cream cheese over each ricecake and top with desired amount of pie filling.
Whip up topping according to directions.
When near the end of whipping stage, slowly add graham wafer crumbs until well mixed.
Place on desired amount on pie filling.
Cool for a few minutes before serving.

Variation: *Before adding whipped topping, heat in microwave for 20-30 seconds EACH.*

Makes 4 - 6 ricecakes

Mincemeat Deluxe

4 - 6	4 - 6	ricecakes
125 ml	1/2 cup	bran or grapenut
250 ml	1 cup	mincemeat
250 ml	1 cup	yogurt

Spread generous amount of mincemeat on ricecake.
Top with 2-3 tablespoons of yogurt.
Sprinkle with bran or grapenut.

Great way to get you moving!
Makes 4 - 6 servings.

Cherry Mincemeat

4 - 6	4 - 6	ricecakes
125 ml	1/2 cup	cherry pie filling
125 ml	1/2 cup	mincemeat
50 ml	1/4 cup	shredded coconut
125 ml	1/2 cup	yogurt
125 ml	1/2 cup	cream cheese
125 ml	1/2 cup	chopped dates

Spread each ricecake with cream cheese.
Top with a thin layer of mincemeat, then cherry
pie filling.
Place a spoonful of yogurt in centre.
Sprinkle with dates and coconut.

Different and delicious!
Makes 4 - 6 ricecakes.

Desserts

Appetizers

We suggest that the ricecake be cut with a long sharp knife. With most of the appetizer recipes the ricecake can be cut after the ingredient has been put on. The best way to cut them is in small pie shapes, usually four pieces to a ricecake.

Bed Of Mussels

5 - 6	5 - 6	ricecakes
104 g	1 3.67 oz can	mussels
50-125 ml	1/4-1/2 cup	finely grated cheese
2 - 3	2 - 3	thinly sliced olives
50 ml	1/4 cup	mayonnaise

Spread butter and mayonnaise on each ricecake.
Sprinkle cheese on evenly.
Top with mussels and a little more cheese.
Garnish with a slice of olive.

Another great party snack!
Makes 16 - 24 appetizers.

Smoked Mussels

4 - 6	4 - 6	ricecakes
105 g	1-3.7 oz	can smoked mussels
6 - 12	6 - 12	sliced olives
50 ml	1/4 cup	tartar sauce
50 ml	1/4 cup	sour cream

Butter and spread tartar sauce on each ricecake.
Place mussels evenly over surface.
Top with olives and a dab of sour cream.

(See "Sauces" section for homemade tartar sauce).

Makes 16 - 24 appetizers.

Appetizers

Smoked Oysters

4 - 6	4 - 6	ricecakes
1 - 104 g	1 - 3 oz can	smoked oysters
2 - 3	2 - 3	hard boiled eggs
25 - 50 ml	2 - 3 tablespoon	tartar sauce
2 - 3	2 - 3	cherry tomatoes
		Vegit

Spread tartar sauce on each ricecake.
Slice hard boiled eggs and place on next.
Top with slices of tomatoes and oysters.
Sprinkle with Vegit.

See "Sauces" section for homemade tartar sauce.

Makes 16 - 24 appetizers.

Shrimp Delight

4 - 6	4 - 6	ricecakes
113 g	1 - 4 oz can	shrimp cocktail
4 - 8	4 - 8	sliced mushrooms
50 ml	1/4 cup	seafood cocktail sauce
50 ml	1/4 cup	caviar

Butter ricecakes and spread on desired amount of seafood sauce.
Place sliced mushrooms evenly on ricecakes.
Top with shrimp and a dab of caviar.

See "Sauces" section for seafood cocktail sauce.

Makes 16 - 20 appetizers.

Pacific - Pilchards

4 - 6	4 - 6	ricecakes
50 ml	1/4 cup	tartar sauce
215 ml	7.6 oz can	Pacific-pilchards (in tomato sauce)
125 ml	1/2 cup	shredded cheese
50 ml	1/4 cup	mayonnaise
		Vegit

Spread each ricecake with mayonnaise.
Top with fish, a dab of tartar sauce.
Cheese and Vegit.

Makes 16 - 24 appetizers.

Hot Smoked Fish

3 - 4	3 - 4	ricecakes
15 ml	1 tablespoon	horseradish sauce
90 g	3 1/4 oz can	smoked fish
2	2	cherry tomatoes
15 m	1 tablespoon	mayonnaise
		garlic powder
		Vegit

Drain fish and mix with horseradish, mayonnaise, pinch of garlic
and Vegit.
Spread mixture evenly over ricecakes.
Top with a slice or two of tomato and Vegit.
To have an extra KICK, add two tablespoons of horseradish
instead of one.
Cut ricecakes into pie-shaped pieces.

Makes 12 - 16 appetizers.

Salmon & Alfalfa Sprouts

4 - 6	4 - 6	ricecakes
1 - 2	1 - 2	sliced hard boiled eggs
1/2	1/2	sliced green pepper
125 ml	1/2 cup	alfalfa sprouts
50 ml	1/4 cup	caviar
2-3 g	7.5 oz can	pink salmon

Sprinkle alfalfa sprouts on buttered ricecakes.
Arrange slices of egg over sprouts.
Top with pink salmon and green pepper.
Dab of caviar to top it off.

Makes 16 - 24 appetizers.

Broccoli Flowerette

4 - 6	4 - 6	ricecakes
1/2	1/2	medium size broccoli
250 g	1/2 lb	Gouda or Monterey Jack cheese

Cover each ricecake with cheese.
Break broccoli into pieces and arrange on cheese.
Top with cheese and heat each ricecake in microwave for 30-50
seconds on HI or until cheese has melted slightly.

Makes 16 - 24 appetizers.

Mackerel Fillets

4 - 6	4 - 6	ricecakes
125 g	5 1/2 oz can	mackerel fillets
2 - 3	2 - 3	shredded lettuce leaves
1	1	thinly sliced cucumber
50 ml	1/4 cup	tartar sauce
		garlic powder

Spread tartar sauce on each ricecake.
Cover with lettuce and top with cucumber.
Drain fish and break into small pieces.
Place fish on cucumber and sprinkle with garlic powder.

Makes 16 - 24 appetizers.

Octopus Garden Delight

4 - 6	4 - 6	ricecakes
4 - 6	4 - 6	sliced olives
115 g	4 oz	can octopus
50 ml	1/4 cup	tartar sauce

Butter each ricecake and spread on tartar sauce.
Place octopus pieces on evenly.
Top with olives and parsley.

Check "Sauces" section for homemade tartar sauce.

Makes 16 - 24 appetizers.

Appetizers

Golden Tamarilos

4 - 6	4 - 6	ricecakes
398 ml	14 oz can	Golden Tamarillos
250 ml	1 cup	yogurt
50 ml	1/4 cup	shredded coconut
50 ml	1/4 cup	caviar
50 ml	1/4 cup	cream cheese
4 - 6 ml	4 - 6	sliced whole cherries

Spread cream cheese on each ricecake.
Place one whole tamarillo in the middle so that it will spread out.
Top with caviar, coconut and cherry slice.

Looks rich and tasty on party table!
Makes 16 - 24 appetizers.

Italian Sardines

4 - 6	4 - 6	ricecakes
15 - 30 ml	1-2 tablespoons	mayonnaise
15 ml	1 tablespoon	Italian dressing
5 ml	1 teaspoon	prepared mustard
100 g	3.53 oz can	sardines
1	1	small finely grated carrot

Mix in bowl: Mayonnaise, Italian dressing, mustard, sardines.
Place mixture on ricecakes and top with grated carrot.

Makes 16 - 24 appetizers.

Sardine Supreme

4 - 6	4 - 6	ricecakes
90 g	3 1/4 oz can	sardines
5 ml	1 teaspoon	parsley
50 ml	1/4 cup	cream cheese
5 ml	1 teaspoon	lemon juice
50 ml	1/4 cup	seafood sauce
		garlic powder

Mix sardines, seafood sauce, lemon juice, and a pinch of garlic powder together.
Spread cream cheese on each ricecake.
Top with sardine mixture and garnish with olives and parsley.
See "Sauces" section for seafood sauce.

Makes 12 - 16 appetizers.

Shrimp Avocado Special

4 - 6	4 - 6	ricecakes
4 - 6	4 - 6	sliced mushrooms
1	1	sliced avocado
113 g	4 oz can	shrimp cocktail
50 ml	1/4 cup	cream cheese
		Vegit

Spread cream cheese on each ricecake.
Cover surface with avocado.
Top with shrimp and mushrooms.
Sprinkle with Vegit.

Great for guests!
Makes 16 - 24 appetizers.

Cheesy Sauce

| 250 ml | 1 cup | mayonnaise |
| 50 ml | 1/4 cup | Blue Cheese Salad Dressing |

Mix mayonnaise and blue cheese salad dressing together.

Variation: If you find the sauce a bit too strong add another 50 ml - (1/4 cup) mayonnaise.

This cheese sauce tastes great over most of the crêpette dishes.

Curry Sauce

250 ml	1 cup	mayonnaise
30 ml	2 tablespoons	Italian Dressing
15 - 30 ml	1- tablespoons	curry powder

Mix all ingredients together in a bowl.
Serve over rice, chicken or any of the salad recipes.

Zesty Mustard Sauce

250 m	1 cup	mayonnaise
15 ml	1 tablespoon	prepared mustard
15 - 30 ml	1-2 tablespoons	Italian Dressing

Mix all ingredients together in a bowl.
Serve over your favourite ricecake dish.

(Remember, you can use Kraft light salad dressing instead of mayonnaise).

Tastes especially great over meat dishes.

Sauces

Caesar's Delightful Sauce

| 125 ml | 1/2 cup | mayonnaise |
| 50 ml | 1/4 cup | Caesar Salad Dressing |

Mix together and serve as topping to almost any recipe calling for meat.

Sweet Sauce

| 125 ml | 1/2 cup | mayonnaise |
| 50 - 125 ml | 1/2 - 1/4 cup | Cole Slaw Salad Dressing |

Mix together and serve on egg or meat dishes. Great for donair recipe.

Note: *There is a cholesterol-free mayonnaise available on the market in most areas.*

Try it in these sauces.

Sweety Pie

1	1	ricecake
125 g	1/4 lb	smarties or similar candy
125 g	1/4 lb	milk chocolate
125 g	1/4 lb	miniature marshmallows

Break chocolate into chunks and place in microwaveable dish.
Heat in microwave for 1-2 minutes on HI or until chocolate has melted.
Stir at least once during melting process.
Pour melted chocolate on piece of wax paper and spread out to make 7'x 7' round shape.
Break ricecake into small pieces and drop into chocolate.
Top with a layer of marshmallows.
Sprinkle with smarties.
Heat in microwave for about 40-50 seconds on HI.
Allow sweety pie to cool until hard.
Place in refrigerator - covered - to speed up process.
Spray pizza cutter with oil and cut into pie shapes or break into bite-size pieces.

Kids parties - what a treat!
Makes one sweety pie.

Children's Favourites

Fluff Marshmallow Treat

1	1	ricecake
		marshmallow fluff
		rainbow sprinkles
		toasted coconut

Spread marshmallow fluff on ricecake.
Top with rainbow sprinkles and coconut.

Simple and sweet!
Makes one serving.

Peanut Butter Twist

1	1	ricecake
		peanut butter
		honey

Spread peanut butter on ricecake.
Top with honey.
Heat in microwave for 20-25 seconds on HI.

Great hit with kids!
Makes one serving.

Toasted Ricecake

1	1	ricecake
		jam, honey or marmalade

Spread butter on ricecake and heat in microwave for
20-30 seconds on HI.
Top with jam, honey or marmalade.

Try this for breakfast!
Makes one serving.

Children's Favourites

Marshmallow Treat

4 - 6	4 - 6	ricecakes
1	1 small pkg	miniature marshmallows
50 ml	1/4 cup	granola
50 ml	1/4 cup	shredded coconut
50 ml	1/4 cup	currants or raisins

Cover surface of ricecakes loosely with marshmallows.
Sprinkle with granola, currants and coconut.
Heat EACH ricecake for 30-60 seconds on HI or until
marshmallows have melted together.
Allow 1-2 minutes cooling time before eating or cool overnight in
refrigerator.

Great school treat!
Makes 4 - 6 servings.

Yogoberry Crunch

4 - 6	4 - 6	ricecakes
750 ml	3 cups	strawberry yogurt
500 ml	2 cups	fresh sliced strawberries
500 ml	2 cups	whipped cream
125 ml	1/2 cup	chopped walnuts
4 - 6	4 - 6	dessert bowls

Break a ricecake into each bowl.
Mix each ricecake with 125 ml or 1/2 cup yogurt.
Top with desired amount of whipped cream.
Sprinkle with chopped walnuts.
Chill for a few minutes before serving.

If you are watching your waistline, try low fat yogurt.

Makes 4 - 6 servings.

Children's Favourites

Marshmallow Bars

The following bars are great tasting and fun to make.

The fruit leather that is mentioned in the recipes can be bought in sheets, e.g. fruit roll-ups

4 - 6	4 - 6	ricecakes
4 - 6	4 - 6	fruit leather sheets
250 ml	1 cup	marshmallow miniatures
125 ml	1/2 cup	sunflower seeds

Place marshmallows on each ricecake loosely.
Sprinkle with sunflower seeds.
Place prepared ricecake on inverted, microwaveable drinking glass.
Top with fruit leather and allow it to hang over edge.
Heat each prepared ricecake in microwave for 60-70 seconds on HI.
Allow a minute to cool and press hanging fruit leather to bottom of ricecake.
Cooling time should be at least 4-5 minutes before eating.

Makes 4 - 6 bars.

Banana Cinnamon Bars

4 - 6	4 - 6	ricecakes
4 - 6	4 - 6	fruit leather slices
2 - 3	2 - 3	sliced bananas
125 ml	1/2 cup	chopped nuts
		cinnamon

Butter ricecakes and sprinkle with cinnamon.
Place banana slices evenly over surface.
Sprinkle on a little more cinnamon and chopped nuts.

See Marshmallow Bars for next two steps in preparing bars.

Granola Bars

4 - 6	4 - 6	ricecakes
4 - 6	4 - 6	sheets fruit leather
125 ml	1/2 cup	granola
125 ml	1/2 cup	peanut butter
		honey

Spread peanut butter on each ricecake.
Top with desired amount of granola and honey.
See Marshmallow Bars for next two steps in preparing bars.

Walnut Date Bars

4 - 6	4 - 6	ricecakes
4 - 6	4 - 6	sheets fruit leather
125 ml	1/2 cup	chopped walnuts
125 ml	1/2 cup	chopped dates
50 ml	1/4 cup	apple butter

Spread apple butter on each ricecake.
Top with walnuts.
See Marshmallow Bars for next two steps.

Fig Nut Bars

4 - 6	4 - 6	ricecakes
4 - 6	4 - 6	fruit leather sheets
125 ml	1/2 cup	chopped almonds or pecans
125 ml	1/2 cup	apple butter
125 ml	1/2 cup	chopped figs

Spread apple butter on each ricecake.
Sprinkle with figs, nuts and a dab of apple butter.
Please see Marshmallow Bars for next two steps.

Makes 4 - 6 bars.

Brandon's Peanut Butter Snack

1	1	ricecake
15 ml	1 tablespoon	granola
15 ml	1 tablespoon	peanut butter

Spread peanut butter on ricecake.
Sprinkle on granola and top with a dab of honey.

Kids love it!
Makes one serving.

Peanut Butter & Banana Whip

4 - 6	4 - 6	ricecakes
1 - 2	1 - 2	diced bananas
50 ml	1/4 cup	peanut butter
125 ml	1/2 cup	whipped topping

Spread peanut butter on each ricecakes.
Top with diced banana and desired amount of whipped topping.
Sprinkle on a bit more bananas.

Great for banana lovers!

Wiz-Kid Celery Snack

4 - 6	4 - 6	ricecakes
125 ml	1/2 cup	cheese whiz
2 - 4	2 - 4	celery stocks
		Veg-sal or salt

Spread generous amount of cheese on each ricecake.
Slice celery and place on ricecake.
Sprinkle with a little Veg-sal.

Great after-school snack.
Makes 4 -6 servings.

Candy Crunch Bars

5 - 7	5 - 7	ricecakes
125 ml	1/2 cup	milk chocolate
125 ml	1/2 cup	chopped peanuts
125 ml	1/2 cup	sprinkles or rainbow coconut

Place chocolate in small microwaveable bowl.
Heat in microwave for 2-3 minutes on HI or until chocolate is smooth and creamy.
Break ricecakes into bite-size pieces and dip into chocolate covering all sides.
Place on wax paper, on flat surface.
Sprinkle with chopped peanuts, sprinkles or coconut.
Allow candy to harden at least 1/2 to a hour in refrigerator.

Great Treat!
Makes several candy pieces.

Peanut Butter & Jam

4 - 6	4 - 6	ricecakes
125 ml	1/2 cup	peanut butter
50 ml	1/4 cup	jam or jelly

Spread generous amount of peanut butter on each ricecake.
Heat in microwave for 20 seconds on HI - EACH.
Remove and top with jam or jelly.
Tastes great warm or cold.

Makes 4 - 6 servings.

Children's Favourites

Ricecake Words

Spread cake frosting on ricecakes.

With cake decorating letters spell out your name or favourite slogan.

Caramel Topping

Spread caramel sunday topping on ricecakes.

Sprinkle with chopped nuts, coconut or snowflakes.

Molasses & Cream Cheese

Spread cream cheese on ricecakes.

Top with desired amount of molasses.

Tic-Tac-Toe

Spread a thin layer of marshmallow fluff on ricecake.

Draw lines with frosting.

Use small candy for playing pieces.

Peanut Fluff-Swhirl

Place desired amount of marshmallow fluff in mixing bowl.

Stir in chopped nuts and your favourite jam.

Spread on ricecake.

Ice Cream Rainbow

1	1	ricecake
		rainbow sprinkles
		ice cream

Place desired amount of ice cream on ricecake.
Spread out to edges and top with nuts and rainbow sprinkles.

Ice cream delight!
Makes one serving.

Yogurt Spread

1	1	ricecake
		yogurt
		coconut

Spread desired amount of yogurt on ricecake.
Sprinkle with coconut.

Eat right away!
Makes one serving.

Children's Favourites

Preparing Basic Crêpettes

1. Eggs for the crêpette have to be prepared one at a time, to do this:

    – Break egg into bowl
    – Add spices that recipe calls for
    – Mix well

2. Take a 7" microwaveable plate and spray with oil.
    Pour in egg mixture and move around plate to allow
    egg to spread out as thin as possible.

3. Place plate in microwave and cook egg for approxi-
    mately 2 minutes on HI turning at least once, or
    until egg is cooked.

4. Carefully remove egg with spatula and lay on flat
    surface until needed.

5. To prepare ricecake, place called for ingredients on surface.
    Fold egg in half, then quarter and place on ricecake.

6. Insert ingredients of recipe into layers of egg topping
    with whatever recipe calls for (cheese, yogurt, etc).

Pizza Crêpette

4 - 6	4 - 6	ricecakes
4 - 6	4 - 6	eggs
250 ml	1 cup	shredded mozzarella cheese
4 - 6	4 - 6	sliced mushrooms
4 - 6	4 - 6	sliced olives
1/2	1/2	diced green pepper
125 ml	1/2 cup	pizza sauce
250 ml	1 cup	sliced pepperoni
		pizza spices
		Vegit

To prepare crêpette see: "Preparing Basic Crêpette".

Sprinkle pizza spices and Vegit into egg mixture.
Place a slice or slices of cheese on ricecakes.
Folded egg goes next.
Insert meat, mushrooms, peppers and desired amount of cheese into layers of egg.
Top with cheese and desired amount of pizza sauce.
Heat in microwave for 40-60 seconds on HI or until heated through and cheese is melting.

Makes 4 - 6 crêpettes.

Ham & Cheese

4 - 6	4 - 6	ricecakes
8 - 12	8 - 12	slices of cheese
4 - 6	4 - 6	slices of cooked ham
125 ml	1/2 cup	diced onion

To prepare crêpette see: "Preparing Basic Crêpette".

Add a little onion, pepper and Vegit to egg mixture before cooking.
Place a slice of cheese on each ricecake.
Top with folded egg.
Insert ham, pepper and cheese into each layer.
Top with a slice of cheese.
Heat in microwave for 40-60 seconds on HI or until heated through and cheese is melting.

Makes 4 - 6 crêpettes

Fruit

4 - 6	4 - 6	ricecakes
4 - 6	4 - 6	eggs
125 ml	1/2 cup	cream cheese
1 - 2	1 - 2	sliced bananas
250 ml	1 cup	yogurt
		cinnamon

To prepare crêpette see: "Preparing Basic Crêpette".

Cover surface of ricecake with cream cheese.
Place folded egg on next.
Insert fruit into each level of egg.
Sprinkle with cinnamon.
Top with yogurt.

Makes 4 - 6 crêpettes.

Cheese

4 - 6	4 - 6	ricecakes
4 - 6	4 - 6	eggs
250 ml	1 cup	shredded cheese

To prepare crêpette see: "Preparing Basic Crêpette".

Place folded egg on ricecake.
Insert cheese into each layer.
Heat in microwave for 40-60 seconds on HI or until cheese is hot and melting slightly.

Makes 4 - 6 crêpettes.

Fish

4 - 6	4 - 6	ricecakes
4 - 6	4 - 6	eggs
8 - 12	8 - 12	slices of cheese
4 - 6	4 - 6	sliced mushrooms
1	1	diced onion
213 g	7.5 oz	can salmon or tuna

To prepare crêpette see: "Preparing Basic Crêpette".

Spread tartar sauce on ricecakes.
Place folded egg on ricecake.
Insert fish, mushrooms, onions into egg levels.
Top with favourite sauce.

Makes 4 - 6 crêpettes.

Crêpettes

Sliced Meat

4 - 6	4 - 6	ricecakes
4 - 6	4 - 6	eggs
8 - 12	8 - 12	slices of cheese
1	1	diced green pepper
1	1	diced onion
4 - 6	4 - 6	sliced mushrooms
8 - 12	8 - 12	slices of cooked meat
125 ml	1/2 cup	sauerkraut

To prepare crêpette see: "Preparing Basic Crêpette".

Cover surface of ricecake with cheese.
Place folded egg on next.
Insert meat, sauerkraut, mushrooms and pepper into each layer.
Top with a slice of cheese and heat in microwave for
40-60 seconds on HI or until heated through.

Makes 4 - 6 crêpettes.

Crêpettes

Super Crêpette

The super crêpette is prepared the same way as the basic crêpette except for the last step. In the following recipes the super crêpette is written out for easy instruction.

Peaches & Cheese

4 - 6	4 - 6	ricecakes
2 - 4	2 - 4	fresh peaches OR
796 ml	28 oz can	sliced peaches
250 - 500 ml	1 - 2 cups	cottage cheese
250 ml	1 cup	yogurt
4 - 6	4 - 6	eggs (for crêpettes)
2 - 4	2 - 4	thinly sliced bananas

To prepare see: "Preparing Basic Crêpette".

Make a super crêpette by:

Placing sliced bananas, then peaches in a 6" round by 1" deep microwaveable dish.
Break ricecake over fruit, evenly as possible.
Spoon in desired amount of yogurt.
Fold egg in half and place on yogurt.
Stuff egg with desired amount of peaches and cottage cheese.
Top with another spoonful of yogurt.
A little of the peach juice may be poured over crêpette, but not too much!

What a lunch, breakfast or dessert!
Fits anyone's diet.
Makes 4 - 6 servings.

Crêpettes

Shrimp or Lobster

4 - 6	4 - 6	ricecakes
4 - 6	4 - 6	eggs (for crêpettes)
125 ml	1/2 cup	grated mozzarella cheese
125 ml	1/2 cup	seafood sauce
250 ml	1 cup	shrimp or lobster
		Vegit
		garlic powder

To prepare crêpette see: "Preparing Basic Crêpette".

Add garlic powder and Vegit to uncooked egg mixture.

Make a super crêpette by:

Placing shrimp or lobster on bottom of a 6"round by 1" deep microwaveable dish.
Break a ricecake over shrimp.
Sprinkle with desired amount of cheese.
Top with egg folded in half.
Stuff with shrimp and cheese.
Pour on desired amount of seafood sauce.

Eat as is or heat in microwave for 40-60 seconds on HI or until cheese is melting.

Seafood lovers delight!
Makes 4 - 6 servings.

Crêpettes

Mixed Vegetable

4 - 6	4 - 6	ricecakes
4 - 8	4 - 8	thinly sliced mushrooms
1	1	sliced medium cucumber
1	1	grated carrot
1	1	sliced sweet pepper
1 - 2	1 - 2 cups	cottage cheese
4 - 6	4 - 6	eggs (for crêpettes)

To prepare crêpette see: **"Preparing Basic Crêpette"** *OR make a super crêpette.*

Place slices of cucumber on bottom of 6" round by 1" deep microwaveable dish.
Dab on some cottage cheese.
Break ricecake into dish.
Fold egg in half, place on ricecake.
Stuff egg with desired amount of cucumber, carrot, mushrooms, pepper and cottage cheese.

Top with your favourite sauce or leave as is.

Either way it's great!
Makes 4 - 6 servings.

Crêpettes

Yogoberry

4 - 6	4 - 6	ricecakes
4 - 6	4 - 6	eggs (for crêpettes)
250 ml	1 cup	blueberries or strawberries
250 ml	1 cup	yogurt
		cinnamon

To prepare crêpette see "Preparing Basic Crêpette".

Sprinkle cinnamon in egg mixture.

Make a Super Crêpette by:

Place berries on bottom of 6" round by 1" deep microwaveable dish.
Break a ricecake over berries, as evenly as possible.
Spoon in desired amount of yogurt.
Top with egg folded in half.
Stuff egg with berries and yogurt.
Try a little more yogurt on top and a sprinkle of cinnamon.

A berry treat!

Index

My Own Recipes

My Own Recipes

My Own Recipes

My Own Recipes

My Own Recipes

My Own Recipes